Holiness

David Runcorn

Vicar of St Stephen's, Ealing

GROVE BOOKS LIMITED
BRAMCOTE NOTTINGHAM NG9 3DS

Contents

Acknowledgements

This booklet began life as a series of addresses given to the Southwell Diocesan Conference at Swanwick in October 1994. It is dedicated with grateful thanks to Bishop Patrick Harris—for the honour of the invitation—and to the people and clergy who brought the subject to life with their generous enthusiasm and participation.

Thanks also to my wife Jackie for her comments and encouragements and to Suzanna Rust for the cover picture.

The Cover Illustration is by Suzanna Rust

First Impression August 1995
ISSN 0262-799X
ISBN 1 85174 296 4

1
Introduction

'What are you speaking about?' asked friends when they heard that I was speaking at a diocesan conference. 'Holiness,' I said. Those who knew me well burst out laughing. Others looked at me with genuine pity. 'But what are you going to *say*?' they asked. The subject was nearly always a conversation stopper. Those reactions are very revealing. Had the conference been on the theme of prayer, Celtic spirituality or healing, for example, people would have responded with immediate interest. It is not that we think holiness is unimportant. But we hang around this word with a mixture of fascination and dread. Our responses to the word 'holy' are complex and contradictory.

Once, while wandering around an old country church, I found myself looking into the worn stone face of someone the guide book told me was a 'Saint.' Very little was known about him. I wondered how they knew. He certainly was very old and had a very long beard which in Church history seems to be be synonymous with great sanctity (and may therefore explain the lack of women saints). I was curious, but his serious, hard eyed face stirred a familiar unease in me. It was the fear that holiness is something harsh involving heroic self-sacrifices. Holiness is not for ordinary people. It cannot, in the end, be friends with earth. It is for a few heroes of faith who leave the rest of us admiring yet feeling condemned—because the fierce, fiery embrace of God upon their lives is clearly out of reach of lesser mortals. Holiness can never be a laughing matter. Saints never smile. No one will ever write a bestseller called 'The Joy of Sanctity.'

It was a relief to discover I was not alone. Many Christians are uneasy with the idea of holiness. The word has been used and abused in the Christian church. Very often one aspect of holiness has been stressed at the expense of others. In my own Christian journey I have been drawn to the sense of mystery and transcendence of the God I meet in traditional Catholic worship. But it easily remains other-worldly. I can understand the the kind of guilty sacramental limbo inhabited by the characters in Graham Greene novels. In the Evangelical tradition I meet the immanence of the holy God in Christ. It was here for the first time I learned to take seriously the practical issues of personal holiness and morality. But these seemed to go with an approach to worship that easily became a kind of sacred chattiness allied with a distrust of sacramental mystery.

I have explored the idea of holiness in groups with the following question: 'You walk into a room full of people and someone points to an individual across the room saying, "That person is very holy." How would you expect them to look or behave and what would your response be to them?'

In the discussion that follows many assumed the saint was male (though I said 'person'). They assumed he will be standing alone. Few felt they would be relaxed with him—'he wouldn't have much small talk.' The majority thought they might talk with him but they would not expect him to be able to understand the issues and problems of their own lives—'he would be "beyond" all that.' The picture of holiness was almost totally negative.

Groups were then asked to describe moments or places when they had felt God very near, or a sense of 'holy' presence. Encounters through nature were the most common—especially moments of unusual stillness and quiet. And the stories nearly always concluded 'and there were no other people for miles around!'

My conviction is that our vision of Christian holiness has got stuck in certain narrow, unimaginative definitions. We are left responding to the word with the formality and enthusiasm we reserve for substances like disinfectant.

That is not the picture of holiness found in the scriptures. Holiness begins and ends in the mystery, wonder, joy and fire of God's love.

2
'Holy, Holy, Holy':
The God of the Old Testament

In the beginning was the Holy. And the holy was God. Without holiness nothing was made that has been made.

Holy Other

'Holy' is the oldest word of all. In any culture or language it is the one that tries to express the mystery of divine presence. The Hebrew word is *qadosh*. It translates 'separate' or 'cut off.' God is 'separate' in the sense of being wholly other than what he has made. Nothing and no one is to be compared with him. Separation is not a negative idea in the Bible. It is central to life. It is through the separation of chaotic elements that creation came into being. When Adam named all creatures he both separated himself and established relationship with them. Adam entered relationship with Eve by first being separated from her (Genesis 2.20ff).

A fierce sense of Holy 'otherness' separated the God of the Israelites from the gods of the surrounding nations. The true God was hidden. He dwelt in cloud and thick darkness (Deuteronomy 4.11-12). It was precisely that he could not be known or seen that marked him out from other false gods (see Isaiah 44.6ff). Images were forbidden. No word or vision could describe him. Such a God was to be feared and held in awe and dread. By contrast the false gods could be seen and touched. They were idols. To see the true God at all was certain destruction (Exodus 33.18-23).

In the Hebrew scriptures *qadosh* became a name almost synonymous with God—'The Holy One.' Holiness is not another attribute of God to be compared with other attributes such as God's compassion, righteousness or mercy. 'Holy' is *the* characteristic of God and sums up all that is different about him, separating him from comparison with any other creatures or divine beings.

'I am God and not man: the Holy One in the midst of you' (Hosea 11.9).

Holy Meeting

The word 'holy' has another Semitic root that is translated 'shining' or 'gleaming.' There is an attraction to and fascination with the 'Holy' that is not the preserve of particularly 'religious' people. It is at the heart of being human, made in the image of God. God has forever marked our experience with a divine restlessness and longing that nothing earthly can ever fulfil.

5

Holiness as we first meet it in the scriptures is therefore a boundary word. It is intended to express the place of meeting. The place is awesome, glorious, terrifying, mysterious and compelling. Holiness is marked by fear and awe. Nevertheless it is by its more negative aspects that the word is understood today. When applied to God it suggests a severe transcendence, distance and judgment of sin. When the word is applied personally people assume it is almost wholly concerned with moral behaviour, sin and guilt. It comes as a surprise to discover that the primary understanding of holiness in the Bible is not a divine preoccupation with morality and sex. Perhaps it is because encounter with the Holy is so frighteningly mysterious and 'other' that religious life is always tempted to reduce it to issues of behaviour and morality so that it can be more easily measured and made 'safe.' But in all the discussions I have taken part in the luminous attractiveness of holiness— the hunger, mystery, wonder and glory—was hardly mentioned. Yet this is where the vision of Holy God begins in the Scriptures.

It is not that such experiences are rare today. Research has shown that many people are aware of having had significant 'spiritual' experiences at times in their lives. But I find that many people instinctively presume that the church would not accept their stories—so they do not bring them. In *The Christlike God* John Taylor offers this telling comment:

'How regrettable it is, that through the centuries the confessional stalls around the walls of many churches have received the secrets of so many sins, and have not been equally available for the confidences of men and women and children who have been overtaken by the ecstasies or insights or consolations that declare the reality of God! Had this other side of personal experience been invited, no doubt there would have been the same amount of fantasy, neurosis and self-advertisement as had always been exhibited in the confessional, and wise priests would have known how to discern and guide, as they had done hitherto. No doubt they would have found the recitals of glory just as repetitive as the catalogues of sin, for the accounts of these intensely personal experiences are uncannily similar. But at least it might have redressed the balance and made the churches everywhere as mindful of divine initiative as of human failure…then the Christian community would present a less mummified face toward the world and might rediscover the more dynamic exploratory view of the knowledge of God which its own scriptures display.'[1]

Holy Fear

Holiness is dangerous and God is to be feared. The Hebrew people were clear about this. God's presence is not to be presumed upon, nor can a peo-

---

1   John V Taylor, *The Christlike God* (SCM, 1992) p 55.

ple enter there without great risk.

When Moses prepared to ascend Mt Sinai to meet God, the people were given very precise instructions about how to behave (Exodus 19.10ff). To meet the holy God, a people must 'separate' themselves—become holy. Holiness here is seen in terms of a relationship rather than a moral quality. The opposite of holy is not unclean or sinful but 'common' (everyday). The common must be consecrated, made holy, in preparation for a meeting with the Holy God. Consecration is also a protection. 'Be careful that you do not go up the mountain or touch the foot of it. Whoever touches the mountain shall surely be put to death'(Exodus 19.12). The people are warned that if they infringe the boundaries set by God 'he will break out against them' (Exodus 20.24). This reverence for boundary is central to holiness and explains the strict emphasis on the need for obedience. Holy people are people of the Law (Torah).

There is a tendency to treat these stories as if they are the mark of a more primitive culture—as if our modern world has grown out of such a crude way of relating to God. The 'fear of the Lord,' like guilt, can all too easily be treated with suspicion as if its explanation lies in psychology rather than theophany.

Yet I recently heard a Christian youth worker from a tough local estate describe the difficulty she had in getting young people to enter church premises. They hung around by the entrance *afraid to go in*. From their own experience they knew very well that this world was full of uncertain and dangerous spiritual, occult and psychic powers. They had good reason to be fearful and cautious on the boundary of holy ground. Is God really any less terrible in his world now than the Israelites first knew him? 'Have you no fear of me? Will you not tremble before me…?' (Jeremiah 5.22). There have been times in the history of the church when the demands of holy living were so forbidding that people put off baptism until their death bed. 'Lord give me holiness—but not yet' was the prayer! The mood is very different today. I struggle to protect families from making holy promises at the baptism of their child, to a God they have no fear of or real interest in.

Fear of God in the Scriptures is not a cringing, neurotic dread. It is a right reverence for God that puts everything in life into its true context. When Moses ministered to the terror of the people at Sinai he said, 'Do not be afraid. God has come to test you, so that the fear of God will be with you to keep you from sinning' (Exodus 21.20). 'The fear of the Lord is *clean*,' says the psalmist (Psalm 19.7, commonly translated 'pure'). The servant of the Lord 'will delight in the fear of the Lord' (Isaiah 11.3).

Fear of the Lord is the beginning of worship. It is life giving. Yet reticence about holy fear is evident in some of the modernizing of Christian hymns. An example is Faber's beautiful hymn 'My God how wonderful thou art.'

7

The fourth verse originally read:
'O how I fear thee living God
With deepest tenderest fears.
And worship thee with trembling hope
And penitential tears.'
In a widely used revision of this hymn this verse now reads:
'O how I love you living God
Who my heart's longing hears
and worship you with certain hope
And penitential tears.'[2]
What is going on here? The trembling, the holy fear, the life of faith is replaced with the language of certainty.

When I went into retreat before being ordained, many friends sent me cards and messages of encouragement. No one prepared me for the fear. For the entire retreat I was gripped by a fear and terror of the call that was upon me and the response being asked of me. I felt like Jacob waking up in the desert and suddenly realizing the enormity of where he was and who was present with him. 'How terrible is this place!' (Genesis 28.17).

I wept and shook with dread at the step I was making. The retreat utterly exhausted me and I went through the ordination service itself in a spiritual daze. All I had were my tears but I could not express them. It is not done in the Church of England. Its traditional worship has always been a refined and carefully passionless experience. Anglican liturgies have never felt the need to include the occasional rubric '*the congregation may now weep without restraint before God.*' Recent controversy over the emotional release that has accompanied the charismatic phenomenon known as the 'Toronto blessing' merely illustrates how out of touch much church worship has been with human longings and passions. We have been repressing them for a long time.

Holy Creation

One Sunday evening in our church there was a confusion over the Old Testament reading. By mistake the reader read a chapter from Leviticus. (That in itself is not surprising. Most churches only read Leviticus by accident.)

We found ourselves receiving long and detailed instructions on how to prepare a bull for sacrifice. As only the day before I had barbecued 60 chicken portions for a baptism party I felt I was listening to a reading from a recipe book by a very ancient ancestor of Delia Smith.

I had to pay more serious attention to the reading however as my prepared sermon was based on a quite different subject! What I caught in a new way was the fervent and costly devotion of those worshippers. Their wor-

---

ship was a sacred drama by which all of life was offered to the glory and honour of God. This sacramental framework gave expression to all aspects of community and individual life—from thank offering for blessings, to harvest thanksgiving, to renewal of covenant and significant anniversaries, to sin and guilt offerings. The separation was an offering for the consecration of the whole. The holy Temple, holy shrines, holy City—expressed the holiness of the whole land. The holy Sabbath was for the hallowing of *all* time to God.

Asked why God appeared to Moses out of a thorn bush, Rabbi Joshua ben Karka replied, 'God spoke to Moses out of a thorn bush to teach you that there is no place where the Shekinah is not, not even a thorn bush.'[3]

In the Bible, holiness is very down to earth. It never becomes an otherworldly pietism. The Holy One is in the midst of all of life. This emphasis directly shaped the development of Christian worship. As Kenneth Leech writes, 'The emphasis on the holiness of places and of material things is a fundamental aspect of Jewish life and of the Christian sacramental theology which developed from it.'[4]

This God, who is Holy Other than anything that is made, is found in the midst of life. 'O Lord, our Lord, how majestic is your name in all the earth' sang the psalmist (Psalm 8.1). 'Holy, Holy, Holy is the Lord Almighty; *the whole earth* is full of his glory,' chanted the Seraphim (Isaiah 6.3). In another psalm the writer almost protests that he cannot escape from God!—'Where can I flee from your presence?' (Psalm 139.7). All creation is called to the worship of God. 'Praise the Lord from the earth, stormy winds that do his bidding, wild animals and all cattle' (Psalm 148.7-10). In Leviticus, rules for holy living and worship are set out in exhaustive detail. Chapters 17-26 are traditionally called 'The Holiness Code.' What is fascinating is the way in which 'sacred' and 'secular' concerns are mixed up. Precise instructions for worship are found alongside rules for personal hygiene, environmental issues, sexual relationships and care for poor and the migrant workers.

But at the same time the cultus held the relationship between the holy God and the everyday in a painful sacred tension. It was not resolved. Examples are the separation of mixed marriages (Ezra 9) and the exclusion of diseased, disabled people and menstruating women from worship (Leviticus 15.25ff and 21.2ff). Holiness, in the Old Testament, was never reconciled to what was common or unclean.

The Holiness Code was in fact very radical and subversive in the ancient world. It was an evangelistic sign. The surrounding pagan religions were basically pantheistic and their gods were worshipped through the life of the seasons with its 'secure, sacral order and its predictable rhythms and cycles.'[5]

---

3   Quoted in John V Taylor *The Primary Vision* (SCM, 1963) p 202.
4   K Leech, *True God* (Sheldon Press, 1985) p 40.   **5** *ibid* p 44.

By becoming God's own possession, separated from the world in a unique relationship, Israel was to be a sign and revelation of the character and ways of the true and holy One. The holiness of the people was to be a witness to the nations.

Holy Prophets

Through the ministry of the prophets the idea of holiness developed in a number of significant ways.

Holiness and Sin

Centuries before, when Yahweh appeared in the burning bush, Moses had to be told to remove his sandals. And his reluctance to accept God's call appeared to stem largely from a concern for his credibility (Exodus 3 and 4).

When Isaiah received the vision of the Lord in the temple he was consumed with terror and the sense of his own sin and of his world. 'Woe is me!' (Isaiah 6). There is a new sense of the terminal effect that sin has upon the people's relationship with God: 'Your sins have hidden his face from you, so that he will not hear you' (Isaiah 59.1-2).

Repentance becomes a vital precondition for renewal. 'If you will repent, I will restore you' (Jeremiah 15.19). Ritual cleansing is not enough. 'Rend your hearts and not your garments' (Joel 2.13).

Yet through these same prophecies the character of the holy God emerges in a new way. God is revealed in most personal and vulnerable language. He is hurt by a people who turn away from him. He grieves over their sin. He yearns. In passionate and dramatic language he appeals to the heavens to witness what has happened. 'Has a nation ever changed its gods? But my people have exchanged their Glory for worthless idols. Be appalled at this, O heavens, and shudder with great horror. They have forsaken me, the spring of living water' (Jeremiah 2.11-13).

Through Hosea he speaks like a deserted marriage partner. The longing is always to be able to avert the pain of coming judgment. His love longs to win out. He waits in vain for a change of heart.

There are times this hope seems impractical. In Jeremiah, the fate of the city hangs on the search for just one righteous person.

'Go up and down the streets of Jerusalem, search through her squares.

If you can find but one person who deals honestly

and seeks the truth I will forgive this city' (Jeremiah 5.1).

At other times the salvation of Israel rests upon the inability of the Holy God, even in the face of sin, to forget his love for them. Through Isaiah God speaks of the maternal bond that binds him to his covenant people.

'Can a mother forget the baby at her breast...?

Though she may forget you I will not forget you!' (Isaiah 49.15).

Holy People

In the period leading up to the exile the prophets were fierce critics of cultic worship of their day and called the people to repentance. To a city oblivious to its real danger, Jeremiah prophesied 'Reform your ways and your actions...Do not trust in deceptive words and say, "This is the temple of the Lord, the temple of the Lord, the temple of the Lord!"' (Jeremiah 7.4). There was always a temptation to presume upon the status of being chosen—a holy people. Jeremiah had to warn the people of Jerusalem against treating the Temple as a guarantee of their safety. Religious buildings and rituals have always had a seductive ability to become substitutes for real faith. But there was no salvation by association with a holy place. People who are focussed on buildings and rituals for their security rather than the living God tend to be sacramentalized rather than evangelized.

The prophets condemned worship and prayer that did not lead directly into social involvement. Holiness could almost be translated 'doing justice.' It was concerned with righteousness of life and human compassion. Where this was ignored God speaks with astonishing bluntness:

'I have had more than enough of your burnt offerings,
...who has asked this of you, this trampling in my courts?
Your incense is detestable to me—I cannot bear your evil assemblies.
When you spread out your hands in prayer...your hands are full of blood.
Seek justice, encourage the oppressed' (Isaiah 1.10-17).

The prophets insisted that holiness must be revealed in the politics, economics and social structures of a people. In fact the requirement of justice stood in judgment over the cultus. The holy God is a God of justice and his people must be also.

In Amos 4, the Lord swears by his holiness as he denounces the rich and powerful for their oppression and corruption. He speaks God's disgust for worship that disregards the poor and his vision for a new society: 'let justice roll on like a river, righteousness like a never-failing stream!' (Amos 5.24).

But the relationship between the ritual/liturgical worship and the charismatic (prophetic) tradition in the Old Testament was not all mutual antagonism. Haggai and the post-exilic prophets were firmly committed to the rebuilding of the Temple and the restoration of sacrificial worship.

Holy World

In the face of unrelenting crisis and the stubborn waywardness of the people the prophets looked backwards and forwards. They looked back to the wilderness wanderings as a kind of golden age of faith. 'When Israel was a child, I loved him and out of Egypt I called my son' (Hosea 11.1).

Addressing a corrupt and 'adulterous' people God speaks with the pain and longing of a deserted partner. 'I am going to allure her; I will lead her into the desert and will speak tenderly to her...then she will sing as in the days of her youth. "In that day," declares the Lord, "you will call me 'my husband'"' (Hosea 2.14-15).

They also looked forward to the 'Day of the Lord'—the time when God would judge and restore his world. A recurring theme is the longing for a time when holiness and knowledge of God would be 'natural' to all.

Jeremiah prophesied of the day when the knowledge of God and his presence will be in be every heart. Sin will not even be remembered. All will know God's ways. 'No longer will a man teach his neighbour saying "Know the Lord," because they will all know me, from the least of them to the greatest' (Jer 31.33-4). And Joel looked forward to the day when God's Spirit would be poured out on all, regardless of age, gender or social status (Joel 2.28ff).

Zechariah saw the day coming when special consecration of the Temple would work in reverse. Ordinary things would be 'naturally' holy. Household objects 'will be like the sacred bowls in front of the altar. Every pot in Jerusalem and Judah will be holy to the Lord Almighty' (14.20f).

Isaiah prophesies of a coming leader, full of God's Spirit, who will lead the whole world into a reign of peace, justice and security. In that world 'the wolf will lie down with the lamb...They will neither hurt nor harm on all my holy mountain, for the earth shall be filled with the knowledge of the Lord, as the waters cover the sea.' (Isaiah 1.6 and 9)

Holy Name

Almost more than any of the prophets Ezekiel was consumed with a sense of Israel's sin. Chapter after chapter warns that the nation has no appeal before their Holy God. Their situation is hopeless. But God *chooses* to save his people. Unlike Hosea or Jeremiah he does not appeal to his love or inability to forget his people. Far from it. 'It is not for your sake, that I am going to do these things, but for the sake of my holy name, which you have profaned among the nations. Then the nations will know that I am the Lord' (Ezekiel 36.22-23). This is no longer because God loves or hurts.

'All of that is spent and forfeit. No appeal to covenant love, pathos or fidelity is made. The holiness of God serves only God. It has no other purpose, no partner to take into account. It enters no other service. It cannot be presumed upon. God's free holiness does not make God indifferent, as we might expect. Instead, God's free holiness presses God to act for the sake of one who evokes no love on God's part. This is good news for extreme situations of failure and profanation!'[6]

6   W Brueggemann, *Hopeful Imagination* (SCM, 1986) pp 79-80.

Holy and Immortal

To confess the holiness of God is therefore to proclaim his complete freedom from all he has made. To be committed to the holy God is therefore to live with a divine insecurity. To be a holy people is be entirely dependent upon God's free disposition towards us. In the final analysis we have no other appeal. This is what his holiness actually means. He is other than us and we must learn not to treat him as a tribal or cultic deity, there to meet our needs and bless our crops.

This is the hardest lesson of all. 'We are so preoccupied with God's relatedness, God being for us, that we do not attend enough to God's own hiddenness.'[7]

The prophet Habbakuk complained to God bitterly about the triumph of the evil and wicked. But in his final prayer of commitment his praise and dedication owes nothing to any sign of God's blessing. The Holy God is to be praised and reverenced for who he is—not for what he does.

'Though the fig-tree does not bud,
and there are no grapes on the vines,
though there are no sheep in the pen
and no cattle in the stalls,
yet I will rejoice in the Lord,
I will be joyful in God my Saviour.' (Habbakuk 3.17-19)

7   *ibid* p 71.

13

3
Holy Disorder:
Jesus and the Gospels

In the coming of Jesus the understanding of holiness is shockingly trans-
formed. Holy separation is now holy incarnation. The Holy has taken flesh.
Holiness has now embraced what is profane (pro-fane: literally 'outside the
Temple'). 'The union of holy and common that is foreshadowed in the Old
Testament [is now fulfilled]. To be holy is not to be separate but to be close.
And the holy and the common are one.'[8]

Holy One

It is clear that encounters with Jesus awakened the same attraction and
dread that marked encounters with the Holy God in the Old Testament.

Although people were irresistibly drawn to him there was an awe-ful
otherness about him that even the disciples never quite came to terms with.
Despite being recognisably the carpenter's son from Nazareth (Mark 6.3), he
spoke and acted with other-worldly wisdom and power. Wonder, astonishment, fear, amazement, terror, astonishment and trembling frequently char-
acterize the effect he had on people. He claimed lordship over the wind and
the waves, and confronted demonic power with absolute authority. Indeed,
the first time he is called 'Holy' in Mark's gospel, it is the confession of a
demon who is promptly silenced and cast out (Mark 1.24).

On one occasion a community was so disturbed by his presence they
asked him to leave (Mark 5.17). The disciples themselves were frequently
overwhelmed in his company. 'They were on their way up to Jerusalem,
with Jesus leading the way, and the disciples were astonished, while those
who followed were afraid.' (Mark 10.32).

Even his resurrection appearances were marked by terror. At the empty
tomb 'trembling an astonishment came upon them, and they said nothing to
anyone, for they were afraid' (Mark 16.8). In the appearances that followed
Jesus had first to minister his peace.

Holy Will

Holiness for Jesus was found primarily in his uncompromising and lov-
ing consecration to the Father's will. He has no other task on earth than to
glorify the Father by speaking his words and doing his works (John 4.34).

---

8   K Leech, *True Prayer* (Sheldon Press, 1986) p 35.

14

Holiness means nothing less than to 'love the Lord your God with all your heart, and with all your soul and with all your mind...[and] love your neighbour as yourself...' (Matthew 22.37).

It requires a loyalty and devotion that take priority over the demands of marriage and family and personal ambition (Luke 14.26). Holiness requires a purity of heart, not just of action. He made the commandments more demanding by insisting the attitude of heart was the same as the action (Matthew 5).

Holiness requires a singleness of heart. Like Mary, it calls for an undistracted focus in the face of many distractions (Luke 10.38-42). Jesus never hides the costliness of this commitment. It is the way of the cross (Luke 14.27).

Jesus taught that a holy community will be like salt in the world. This is both a positive and negative calling. Salt flavours and stimulates. It also preserves and disinfects. Christian holiness is therefore found in *closer* involvement with the corruption and decay of the world. Christian holiness is 'in touch' with the profane.

Holy Trust

Jesus used children to illustrate the kind of faith and trust that finds the Kingdom. In his book on prayer, Simon Tugwell makes an important connection between holiness and becoming like a child. This is unexpected because we tend to think holiness involves an adult seriousness of purpose. But true holiness, he suggests, involves letting go of trying to be God. It involves abandoning the search for our own sanctification and living in the freedom of childlike trust. 'Becoming as a little child means unlearning the false solemnity of adolescence, unlearning the false maturity and self importance of ideology and puritanism. It means forgetting to run the world, forgetting to run one another's lives. It means forgetting even to run our own lives.'[9]

Holy trust is marked by joy and freedom—even carelessness (see Philippians 4.6, 'be careful for nothing'). When Jesus spoke of the life of the Kingdom he frequently told stories of wedding receptions, banquets and joyful celebrations.The holy lifestyle of Jesus was so exuberant and generous that his drinking, partying and the company he kept caused scandal among his critics (Matthew 11.19). It is even said that he endured the cross for the joy that was set before him (Hebrews 12.2).

Worldly Holiness

The real scandal of God's holiness in the gospels was that it kept falling into the wrong hands! Nowhere is this clearer than when Jesus says to the

---

9 S Tugwell, *Prayer—Volume 1 Living with God* (Veritas, 1974) p 39.

Pharisees (literally 'separated ones'), 'I tell you the truth, the tax collectors and the prostitutes are entering the kingdom of God ahead of you' (Matthew 21.31).

What is clear from the ministry of Jesus is that 'goodness' is at least as dangerous as sin and evil. It was the 'holy' and 'good' religious devotion that brought him to the cross. There can be nothing more damning for a religion than that it should end up executing God in the name of God. Holiness is a dangerous pursuit. It may even be bad for you.

In many of Jesus's parables and meetings he carefully addresses two groups of people in his audience—the 'holy' (usually the Pharisees) and the 'profane' (tax collectors and 'sinners'). For his hearers the stories always had a sting in the tail and the outcome was the reverse of what they would have predicted.

For example Jesus told a story of a father with *two* sons to the usual split audience (Luke 15). One took his inheritance and wasted it in sinful living before repenting and coming home to wild celebration. The other son stays at home and keeps himself separate from all wrong doing. He reveals a loveless, grudging and bitter approach to life and excluded himself from the celebration of his father's love. The story is universally known as the parable of the prodigal son. Why? The story contains a frightening warning about the dangers of religious goodness. The Christian church betrays very careless reading when it persists in naming the story after the 'sinner.'

The same tendency is found in the traumatic incident of the woman dragged into the presence of Jesus by Pharisees (John 8). I cannot help wondering if this story would find a modern application in the attitude of those who wish to 'out' certain church leaders for their alleged homosexual orientation, and have their 'sin' publicly condemned. There seems to be a certainty as to where Jesus would recognize the 'real' wrong in the situation, which this story dramatically warns against.

The church always describes this incident as 'the woman taken in adultery.' Jesus does not choose to address the issue of sexual sin and when he speaks to the women later it is privately, with firm but infinite compassion. What Jesus actually condemned was the men taken in hypocrisy. Godliness and godlessness are not always where we expect to find them.

Humane Holiness

The most attractive quality of the holiness of Jesus was the compassion that flowed from him. Jesus strongly condemned any approach to holiness that amounted to spiritual self-preservation. He had no time for a view of sanctity that was based on ritual and ceremonial fidelity rather than devotion of the heart and human compassion. He condemned a view of holiness that left people impossibly burdened. I have often wondered how Jesus ministered to people left exhausted by the burden of religion that only leaves guilt and condemnation. In my experience the weariness is hard to reach and the natural reluctance to draw near to God again is hard to overcome. To such people Jesus contrasts the 'burden' of vocation to him with this beautiful invitation—'Come to me all who are weary and heavy laden and I will give you rest. Take my yoke upon you and learn from me, for I am gentle and humble in heart and you will find rest for your souls. For my yoke is easy and my burden is light' (Matthew 11.28-30). We do not readily associate holiness with rest.

Jesus constantly refused to be bound by the laws of ritual purity and constantly strayed across social boundaries in a way that caused scandal (for example in John 4.27). In the story of the Good Samaritan he pictures religious people ignoring human suffering to preserve their own ritual purity. He attacks both racial and ritual prejudice that led to loveless separation (Luke 10).

At points where the interpretation of the Levitical Holiness Code was most pitiless in its consequence Jesus brought instead a liberating vision of divine love. A moving example is the ministry of Jesus to the woman suffering from long term bleeding (Luke 8.40-48). Under the teachings of the Holiness Code this woman was ritually unclean. The real issue is more than social hygiene. It has to do with the the holiness of God.

The Levitical line of thought went like this: God is holy and can only be worshipped by what is holy. God is complete in himself and therefore what is offered to him must be whole and unblemished. What is bleeding or diseased represents a diminishment of life, as blood is the carrier of life.The shedding of blood is therefore the great unclean—the antithesis of God. It represents death not life (as life is draining away). God is life, and death is outside God.[10]

The human consequence of such laws surfaces in the desperate story of this woman. For twelve years she had not only suffered from an exhausting medical complaint, she had lived in total spiritual, social and emotional isolation from her community. She now risked everything to secretly touch the cloak of Jesus. Not only was her 'profane' touch recognized and accepted by Jesus, she was healed and her faith commended.

Holy Cross
The Christian faith has lived with the sign of the cross for so long we have ceased to realize the scandal of it. To preach Christ is one thing. To preach Christ crucified on a cross is quite another. It was an appalling,

---

10 I am indebted to the Rev'd Jackie Searle for her unpublished essay '*The importance of purification in priestly cultic writings.*'

blasphemous idea to the Jews, and philosophical nonsense to the Greeks (1 Corinthians 1.23).

The resolution of the divide between the Holy God and this sinful world involves a gift of God so contradictory that New Testament writers pile up the paradoxes in the struggle to express what God has done. 'God was reconciling the world to himself in Christ, not counting men's sins against them. God made him who had no sin to be sin for us...' (2 Cor 5.20, 21).

In the letter to the Hebrews, the church is called to a new separation. Reminding the readers that after the sacrifice for sin the sacrificed bodies are taken outside the camp and burned, he recalls the death of Jesus outside the city. 'Jesus also suffered outside the city gate to make the people holy through his own blood. Let us, then, go to him outside the camp, bearing the disgrace he bore. For here we do not have an enduring city, but we are looking for the city that is to come' (Hebrews 13.11-14).

The death of Christ is the final death of the old code of ritual separation. In the very moment of his death, in the place of the outcast and the cursed, the veil of the Temple was torn *from top to bottom* (Mark 15.38). The holiest place of God lies open to what is common and the ultimate unclean—death— is embraced by a holy God. For the Christian church, holiness will always found on the edge of scandal.

4

Holy Communion:
The Church, the Spirit and the Hope of the Kingdom

I occasionally run a workshop which explores people's personal picture of God. From a list of the main Bible names of God—Lord, Saviour, Father, King, Judge—participants indicate whether each name means 'a lot,' 'something' or 'very little.' On another sheet the main names of ourselves before God are listed—son/daughter, sinner, servant, child—and the same selections are made. When choices are totalled up the picture of God that emerges is discussed. On nearly every occasion the strongest two personal pictures are 'child' and 'sinner.' Bottom of the personal list comes 'saint' (the word means 'holy').

Yet 'saint' was St Paul's favourite way of addressing fellow Christians (see, for instance, Ephesians 1.1). But as his letters make very clear the name did not imply high moral sanctity or spiritual attainment. As in the Old Testament the word first of all refers to a relationship, not any base level of moral purity. It was a gift of grace.

'The Church is holy not because it is a gathering of the good and well-behaved people, but because it speaks of the triumph of grace in the coming together of strangers and sinners who, miraculously, trust one another enough to join in common repentance and common praise—to express a deep and elusive unity in Jesus Christ, who is our righteousness and sanctification.'[11]

This was the experience of the New Testament church.

Holy Wonder

'The New Testament breathes an air of astonishment,' wrote Philip Seddon. 'Travellers emerging from a dark night into the brilliance of a long-awaited day, spellbound by God's inexpressible gift of himself.'[12] The life of the church was a gift of sheer extravagance, made known in the overwhelming presence of the Holy Spirit. In the letter to the Ephesians, Paul describes the gift of the Spirit as a 'seal' and 'guarantee' (Greek: *arrabon*) of an inheritance that has scarcely been imagined (1.13f). In modern Greek the word means engagement ring. To be a holy people is first and foremost to be a community caught up in celebrating the most mysterious, joyful and undeserved betrothal gift of God himself. Holiness is a gift to be celebrated.

All Christian worship involves an entering into holy mystery. Worship ministers firstly to God, not to us. This priority is in danger of being lost in the present enthusiasm for making church services more 'relevant' and 'seeker friendly' (though I think the discussion is very important). Asked why his church used incense, a priest replied, 'Because you can't get it at Marks and Spencers.' Worship must always minister a sense of God's otherness.

Holy and Profane

'Holiness' was the critical issue in the first crisis to hit the New Testament church. The problem was not one of morality but *mission*. Peter had a dream at Joppa. It was in fact a nightmare. He was confronted with everything his Jewish faith had told him was ritually unclean and told to eat. He refused but was rebuked: 'Do not call anything impure that God has made clean.' On waking, he was invited to the house of a Gentile where the Holy Spirit fell in dramatic power on non-Jewish believers (Acts 10). When the church demanded an explanation his appeal was disarmingly simple. 'As I began to speak, the Holy Spirit came on them as he had come on us at the beginning...who was I to think that I could oppose God' (Acts 11.15ff).

---

11 R Williams, *Open to Judgment* (DLT, 1994) p 136.
12 P Seddon, *Darkness* (Grove Spirituality Booklet No 5).

The story highlights three particular aspects to the Christian understanding of holiness.

a) Holiness is firstly the initiative of the holy God. It is not defined or measured in terms of human activity. Without that divine initiative the church may have remained stuck as a Jewish sect.

b) Holiness is no longer defined by a particular rituals or holiness codes, but as life in the Holy Spirit. God and Christ are rarely described as holy at all in the New Testament; the title is reserved for the Holy Spirit. Holiness is therefore prophetic and charismatic. There are signs that the early church found this uncertain and fiery life too uncomfortable to live with. So has every generation of the church since. How much safer to organize religion around special seasons, days and festivals (Galatians 4.10).

c) Christian holiness is about union not separation. Although the word is popularly understood in terms of abstinence and denial, New Testament holiness may be better understood in terms of immersion and transfiguring. Holiness meant living in the world the way Jesus did. And he expressed the holiness of God in the midst of what was profane, unclean and unlovely—ungodly. He united what had been separated.

In practice most of us do the opposite. We operate with an unofficial Levitical code, a kind of spiritual apartheid. We separate life into holy and unholy, sacred and secular—sanctuary not supermarket, pulpits not pubs, worship not work. God is closer in 'nature' than in the cities. Certain types of people are (probably) closer to God than others. Our approach to holiness reveals as much about our prejudices and politics as about the character of God. 'When I feed the poor they call me a saint,' said Dom Helder Camara, 'when I ask why the poor are hungry they call me a communist.'

Christian holiness does not live to itself. In fact holiness is never spoken of in terms of individual sanctity in the New Testament. It is applied to community life—'you are a holy nation' (1 Peter 2.9). The practice of honouring *individual* saints in the church may be quite unhelpful in this respect.

Nor is holiness to be measured by our assumptions of religious dignity, reverence and beauty. It may be very noisy and untidy. I recently heard someone speaking of their experience in a church that had been witnessing dramatic charismatic phenomena. Under the power of the Spirit he had spent long periods of time laughing loudly and uncontrollably, falling to the floor and shaking wildly. Asked what he felt God had been doing he smiled and said, 'He took away my dignity.' But he was not speaking of humiliation. He was speaking as if God had removed a great burden from him. One of the great gifts of the present disturbing renewal of the Spirit is that our most basic assumptions are challenged. Perhaps God does not share the reserve of the British. In common with many neighbouring cultures, he may find us boringly stuffy and pompous!

Likewise, what makes a building 'holy' is its association with prayer and the telling of the gospel of Christ. It may not be especially beautiful. What we consider to be the 'beauty of holiness' may often be the holiness of beauty. The holiness of a building has nothing to do with the splendour of its architecture. What we assume to be holy worship will also be a reflection of our cultural preferences and prejudices. Holiness is not another word for good taste. We learn from the ministry of Jesus that what looks holy may turn out to be quite the opposite—true holiness is found in very unexpected places.

Holy Fire

Christian life is highly inflammable (though its disciplines are easily adapted for fire *prevention*!). A disciple went to Abba Joseph and said to him, 'As far as I can I say my little office, I fast a little, I pray and meditate, I live in peace, I purify my thoughts. What else can I do?' The old man stood up and stretched his hands toward heavens. His fingers became like ten lamps of fire and he said to him, 'If you will, you can become all flame.'[13] Holiness is forged in the consuming fire of God (Hebrews 12.29). It is a fire that inflames love and devotion and burns away what is impure; it both consumes adn tranfigures. St Paul warned believers to be careful how they built their lives because their work would be tested by the fire of God (1 Corinthians 3.10ff). The saints and mystics of the church often spoke of the longing for prayer as like hidden fire within them. To be drawn into contemplation of God was to be held, like base metal, in the fire of divine love. A common comparison is with the burning bush. 'Rejoicing at once and trembling, I who am straw receive the Fire. And, strange wonder! I am incffably refreshed, as the bush of old which burned yet was not consumed.'[14]

Holy Embodiment

'God's desire is revealed in our body,' wrote Rubem Alves. Christian faith is incarnate. It is called, in Christ, to take flesh, not abdicate it. But traditional Christianity has often had a negative attitude to the body. Influenced originally by Greek philosophy a dualism has influenced Christian theology that it has yet to renounce. The split is between flesh and matter (negative) and spirit (my 'true' self). Christian life is understood as the realm of the spirit. The body is therefore an enemy of spiritual life. 'Saints' are those people who have somehow transcended this fleshly world and are now 'spiritual' people. 'Holiness is tantamount to bodilessness and saints are sexless people, mystically attuned to a life transcending earthly matter.'[15]

---

13 Benedicta Ward SLG, *Sayings of the Desert Fathers* (Mowbray, 1981) p 103.
14 Leech, *op cit* pp 38-9.
15 J Nelson, *The Intimate Connection—Male sexuality, Masculine spirituality* (SPCK, 1992) p 23.

In practice this vision of holiness led to the subjugation of women in the church, for in the 'earthiness' of child bearing alone they embodied a reminder of human passions yet to be conquered. Gender has always been a factor in the recognition of sanctity. The Anglican calendar of saints contains 66 men and only seven women.

This dualism is found nowhere in the New Testament. Christian holiness is never rejection of the flesh. Rather, it rejoices in the hope of its transfiguring.

Passionate Holiness

In *Transformed by Love* Sr Margaret Magdalene writes 'There seem to be all too many Christians who are unable to come to terms with, let alone celebrate, their earthiness; they are trapped in a way of thinking that cannot deal with the holiness of sexuality.'[16] This is very important for one basic reason. Without the energy of our passions, we will not have the strength for holiness. 'There is in passion a power that holiness needs.'[17] If we seek goodness only by a suppression and denial of what we consider 'bad' within us we will end up exhausted. Our deepest and most creative energies are often locked up in what we presume to be the 'darker,' less acceptable side.

Have you noticed how the idea of goodness is never as exciting, daring and energetic as our idea of wrong? After a fast and aggressive spell of bowling in a cricket match the captain came over to me and said, 'Well done Dave! You were bowling like a demon!' He then remembered he was talking to a clergyman and was overcome with embarrassment. But why is no adequate compliment available in heaven for a fast bowler in form? Our vision of holiness, sanctification, goodness needs much more vitality and daring. Holiness is not found in safety, innocence and denial. In one astonishing passage of teaching Jesus himself told his followers to be 'shrewd as snakes and innocent as doves' (Matthew 10.16).

In the journey into maturity this is a basic human dilemma. Anyone involved in counselling or the ministry of confession and absolution knows the need to distinguish between true and false guilt. Within the category of false guilt I include struggles, personality or relationships that need facing and accepting rather than rejecting.

Holiness and Mercy

Holiness is involved with sin. It has to be, for
'...holiness belongs primarily to this world. It bears witness that the life

---

16 Margaret Magdalene CSMV, *Transformed by Love—the Way of Mary Magdalene* (DLT, 1989) p 13. This book is a wonderfully helpful reflection on the difficult and neglected task of integrating humanity, sexuality and spirituality in Christ. For further reading see also James Nelson, footnote 14.
17 *ibid* p 10.

we live on earth, a bodily life with all its weakness and pettiness, is yet capable of receiving the rays of supernatural light and of taking on a new and transcendent meaning. This teaches us not merely to endure life, but to desire and even to love it...'[18]

To live in such a world requires discipline. 'Work out your salvation in fear and trembling, for it is God who works in you...' (Philippians 2.12-13). The early church called its members to the highest moral standards. They were warned against presuming upon the grace of God lest they fall under his judgment (Hebrews 10.29ff, 1 Corinthians 11.27).

Yet the ministry to sinners is marked by a firm gentleness that comes from sharing the same frailty. 'If someone is caught in a sin, you who are spiritual should restore him gently. But watch yourself, or you also may be tempted' (Galatians 6.1).

Holiness is not to be confused with perfection (the word 'perfect' is not often the best translation when used in the New Testament; see, for example Matthew 5.48). The saints are not the most perfect, but the most forgiven.

'A human being is holy not because he or she triumphs by willpower over guilt and leads a flawless life, but because that life shows the victory of God's faithfulness *in the midst* of disorder and imperfection. Humanly speaking, holiness is always like this: God's endurance in the middle of our refusal of him, his capacity to meet every refusal with the gift of himself.'[19]

The emphasis is not finally on the sin or the sinner, but on God's forgiveness.

Dietrich Bonhoeffer wrote that the church only becomes a Christian community when it ceases to be the church of the 'devout'—'good' and 'respectable,' and discovers it is the church of the *un*devout—forgiven sinners, living in divine mercy.[20] The extraordinary hope of the gospel is that in our worst, not our best, is found an amazing revelation of love. 'O Happy Fault!—that won for us so great a salvation,' is the astonishing shout of joy in the Easter liturgy. 'Rejoice every time you find an imperfection!' wrote Jean Pierre de Caussade, in an era of severe spiritual disciplines. Why? Because you have another opportunity to receive God's grace. St Paul emphasized this so strongly that he felt he had to warn his readers not to presume upon it. 'Shall we go on sinning, so that grace may increase? By no means!' (Romans 6.1).

Holiness then is the humility to know oneself forgiven and learning the childlike freedom of being loved and not condemned. 'Holiness' wrote Dom Helder Camara, 'is not never falling down. It is getting up again every time you fall, with humility and joy and saying to God, "Yes Lord, I have fallen a hundred times, but thanks to you I have got up a hundred and one times!"'

18 Louis Lavelle, quoted in Margaret Magadalene *op cit* p 6.
19 Williams, *op cit* p 136.
20 D Bonhoeffer, *Life Together* (SCM, 1981) p 86ff.

Holiness and Wholeness

Holiness is not to be confused with personal fulfilment. Holiness is not healthiness nor worship another word for 'workout.' And Jesus flatly contradicts modern assumptions about wholeness: 'Better to enter life maimed than go to hell with two hands' (Mark 9.43). Holiness belongs to God and gives back to God what is his own. It insists that all of life is for the greater 'wholiness' of his glory and kingdom. To pray for God's name to be hallowed on earth is not first of all to ask for our fulfilling in God, 'but the sanctification of God, through the world.'[21]

Christian holiness is the way of the cross and, thus, the way of glory. It involves the willingness to embrace, in Christ, all that is broken, incomplete and unholy in the world. It means fighting evil and refusing sin. Holy living may not be marked with any outward sign of blessing. We should not be surprised to find that many of the saints who most reflect the love of Christ were themselves full of personal struggle and unhealed wounds.

'We have this treasure in jars of clay to show that this all surpassing power is from God and not from us. We are hard pressed on every side, but not crushed, struck down but not destroyed. We always carry around in our body the death of Jesus, so that the life of Jesus may also be revealed in our body. So then, death is at work in us, but life is at work in you' (2 Cor 4.8-12). Holiness then is not an escape from despair, weakness and defeat. Rather they are essential ingredients in the journey into sanctification. We must come to despair of our own attempts at holiness and abandon ourselves to divine grace. Christian holiness is expressed in our incompleteness, not our perfection. We are insecure with this truth though and very easily demand a holiness (or wholeness) of others that is based on unease with our own incompleteness. We cannot require of each other a 'wholeness' that is not yet given. We need a holiness for the 'grey areas.' How accurately we ever recognize holiness in this world is an open question. It may be that most of the real saints, and their communities have yet to be recognized—except by God.

Why do we put ourselves through all this? Because in the end there is no other journey to make. Holiness is the way of truth and life. So in the end, says Leon Bloy, 'There is but one sadness—that of not being a saint.'

In the midst of this fragmented, broken and unfinished world, the holy church, alive in the fire of the Spirit, keeps vigil beside a hope we can never abandon. It is the hope of our transfiguring into the holiness of God.

'My dear friends, we are already God's children, but what we shall be in the future has not yet been revealed (but) when he appears we shall be like him, because we shall see him as he is. Whoever treasures this hope in him, purifies himself, just as he is pure' (1 John 3.2-3).

Holiness means trusting to God the secret of who we are becoming.

---

21 *Dictionary of New Testament Theology Vol 2* (Paternoster Press) p 229.